Izzie Did It!

(I may have helped.)

From the Adventures of Maxie and Izzie

Written and Illustrated by Jane Ferguson

Hi! I'm Maxine but everyone calls me Maxie.

Isabella is my sister and every-one calls her Izzie.

We are best friends. We do
everything together. We eat together.

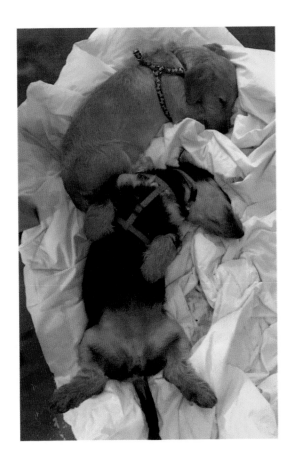

And we
sleep
together.

We love to play

and wrestle together.

We even watch TV together!

We love dog shows best!

But, most of all, we love, love, love to chew, chew, chew! When we were little puppies, our mom bought us tons of toys and bones and chewies.

But sometimes we found our own stuff to chew!

Izzie loved to chew paper but I preferred sandals.

Mom bought us lots of stuff to chew so we wouldn't get into trouble chewing her things. She bought us bones, dental treats, chews and lots more.

You name it, the delivery man brought it to our door.

But one day . . . OH NO!

Izzie discovered she could chew a
TABLE LEG! (I may have helped.)

GUESS WHAT?

Dad got real angry.

Mom bought more chews. They tasted real good.

But one day . . . OH NO!

Izzie discovered Dad's sandals and Mom's tennis shoes and she started chewing. (I may have helped.)

DAD'S SANDAL

mom's SANDAL

mom's SNEAKER

GUESS WHAT?

Mom got real angry and sent us to "time out" in the laundry room where we had our bed. It was real cozy in there. We would snuggle together in our bed and take a nap. We felt sad because Mom was angry.

It's really hard for little puppies to stop chewing.

Mom ordered bigger bones for us. They were delicious. We just chewed and chewed all day long.

Did I tell you that we are real good jumpers? We love jumping on the family room table when Mom is gone.

But one day . . . OH NO!
Izzie chewed Mom's new book.
(I may have helped.)

GUESS WHAT? "Time out" again!
Mom put us back in the laundry room.

But . . . OH NO!
Izzie wasn't tired so she dug a hole in
the wall. It looked like fun. (I may
have helped.)

GUESS WHAT? Dad got real angry. He made up words we never heard before!

Dad said: "This HAS to stop!" He bought two crates for us to sleep in and signed us up for Puppy School. Mom hooked our crates together so we wouldn't get lonely. We share a patio!

Mom bought more bones and chews plus new harnesses and leashes so we'd look good on the first day of school.

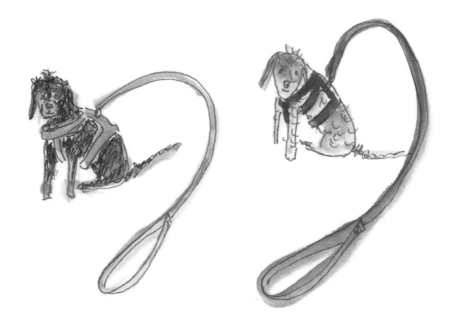

But . . . OH NO!

I don't think Izzie liked her red harness. She chewed the straps right off that red harness. I should have reminded mom that Izzie's favorite color is blue.

GUESS WHAT?

The first day of school was real fun. Izzie had to wear her old blue harness but no one noticed. I wore my new green harness. It's very pretty. We made new friends at school and got lots of treats just for sitting down! We love puppy school!

I don't know if I told you this.
We love the delivery man. Almost
every week he brings us chews and
treats and bones. They are all
delicious.

But one day . . . OH NO!

Izzie discovered Mom and Dad's eye glasses on a table. Do you know how much fun it is to chew eye glasses? (I may have helped.)

GUESS WHAT?

"Time out" again! Mom put us on the porch and told us to be good. Izzie and I were chasing lizards and flies. It was very fun. We had a lizard trapped near the screen and Izzie leaped. She's a real good leaper.

But . . . OH NO!

She leaped right into the screen and accidentally tore a hole in it.

DO YOU KNOW WHAT? That sneaky lizard escaped and when she went after it the screen hole just got bigger and bigger. (I may have helped.)

ESCAPED LIZARD →

GUESS WHAT?

When Dad saw that hole in the screen he got real angry again and said words we've never heard before.

We think he's bilingual. Do you know what that means? He speaks two languages. English and Anger-lish. Our Dad is brilliant!

GUESS WHAT ELSE?

He put us into our sleeping crates—
during the day. We felt sad. We were
trying to be good puppies. It's just that
sometimes we forget.

We were so tired after a long morning of
chasing lizards that we fell asleep
together.

One day mom took us down to her art studio. She made a giant indoor run just for us so we could play there when she's painting and not get into trouble. It was great.

But one day . . . OH NO!

When mom was out of the room, Izzie woke up early from her nap and opened the run door. (I may have helped.). We found mom's red paint tube and brushes. Izzie bit into the paint tube and red paint squirted out everywhere. We were very red puppies!

Mom got real angry and started speaking that strange language that dad taught her. We think mom is bilingual too!

GUESS WHAT?

Mom ordered more chews and we got "time out" again!

One day Izzie and I were playing with our toys. After a while we got tired and took a nap right on our very favorite quilt.

Izzie woke up early and started chewing the buttons off the quilt. That's when we discovered a little hole in the quilt.

But . . . OH NO!

Izzie saw that wonderful white stuffing that she loves and she just couldn't stop herself. (I may have helped.). We pulled all the stuffing out of that beautiful quilt and that little hole just got bigger and bigger. White fluffy stuffing was everywhere. We were covered in it.

GUESS WHAT?

Dad threw away our favorite quilt just because it was all ripped up and unstuffed.

But . . . OH NO!   Mom said: "I give up."

She called a dog trainer. She said we needed to learn some manners or we were going to "Boot Camp!"

We are not sure exactly what manners are but it sounds serious. I'll take good notes and let you know.

Well, I've got to go now. I hope Mom and Dad like this surprise we left. It was Izzie's idea! (I may have helped.)

Xoxoxox,   Maxie

These are the true stories of two cute puppies going through their "terrible chews."

You will be happy to know that we all survived though there were some very "iffy" days when we were questioning our sanity. I can't tell you how many times my husband and I said, "It's a good thing those girls are cute and sweet and oh so lovable!"

Please join us in the continuing adventures of Izzie and Maxie as they discover the world around them, make friends with their neighbors and eventually begin their training to become Therapy Dogs.

This book is dedicated to my grandsons:

Harrison
Noah
Oliver
James

Made in the USA
Lexington, KY
23 July 2017